LUCY CHEN

Reconnect with Your Intelligent and Classy Inner Self Through Art

A Step-by-Step Demo to Painting an Impressionist Style Self Portrait in Three Hours or Less

LUCY CHEN

http://lucychenfineart.com

Cover design by: Lucy Chen

Interior design by: Lucy Chen

Photography by: Lucy Chen

ISBN-10: 1514698498

ISBN-13: 978-1514698495

Your Free Gift

As a way of saying thanks to your purchase, I'm offering a bunch of free bonus art videos that's exclusive to my readers.

You will see my different methods of making an oil painting in these videos. And my progress. And changes in the way I make a painting.

You can watch these videos by going here:

http://bit.ly/lcbook-bonus

Contents

Foreword

I looked around. I was trapped. Trapped in a small room of a big house. The bedroom door was open, but he was blocking it.

But there was another way out. The only way – the shiny object on my desk was calling me to carry out what I had fantasised many times in my mind.

I turned to it, grabbed the Stanley knife, slid out the blade, and slit my left forearm. There was blood, and raw flesh.

I was depressed and deeply unhappy. I hated my marriage. I hated my life. And who could I blame but myself? I did not marry for love. I did not even marry for money. God dammit!

Now I suffered the consequences – already a mother of two little toddlers, it was too late to leave. I hated myself.

After the doctor stitched me up, I spent months questioning, searching, trembling, crying – occasionally in a psychologist's office, and often curled up in the small spare closet, sandwiched between my canvases.

I had long lost touch with who I was. Worse, I had allowed myself to be defined as "insecure", "insensitive", "inconsiderate", and "incapable" amongst many other great qualities.

I tried to dodge the daggers. I tried to defend myself. I fought back. But the toxic fume was in the air. It sank deeper and deeper into the core, aiming for a kill.

No!

I had to get out! I had to. I had to for my children. I had to for my art. I had to, for myself.

It was then that I read Viktor Frankl's Man's Search for Meaning. I'm not saying my self-pity can be any way compared to the great suffering he went through in the Auschwitz concentration camp, but the book's message nevertheless strike a cord with me.

Frankl said, "... everything can be taken from a man but on thing: the last of human freedom - to choose ones own attitude in any given set of circumstances - to choose one's own way."

I had a place to live. I had warm blankets. I had two beautiful children. I had my art. And I could even say I had some talent. What I did not have, what I had lost, was myself.

And it was time that I chose my own way, back to myself.

The Mirror

One of my favourites quotes was from George Bernard Shaw. He said, "You use a glass mirror to see your face; you use works of art to see your soul."

During the months of my recovery, I stumbled on Susannah Conway's The Sacred Alone e-course. It was a 14 day journey back to yourself through journaling combined with bit-sized meditation - just what I needed.

One of the meditations in the course was a "mirror meditation".

You start by looking at yourself in a mirror. Imagine the face you're looking at turn into someone you love. For example, your child. Imagine seeing their contour, their features, and tell your loved one repeatedly, "I love you."

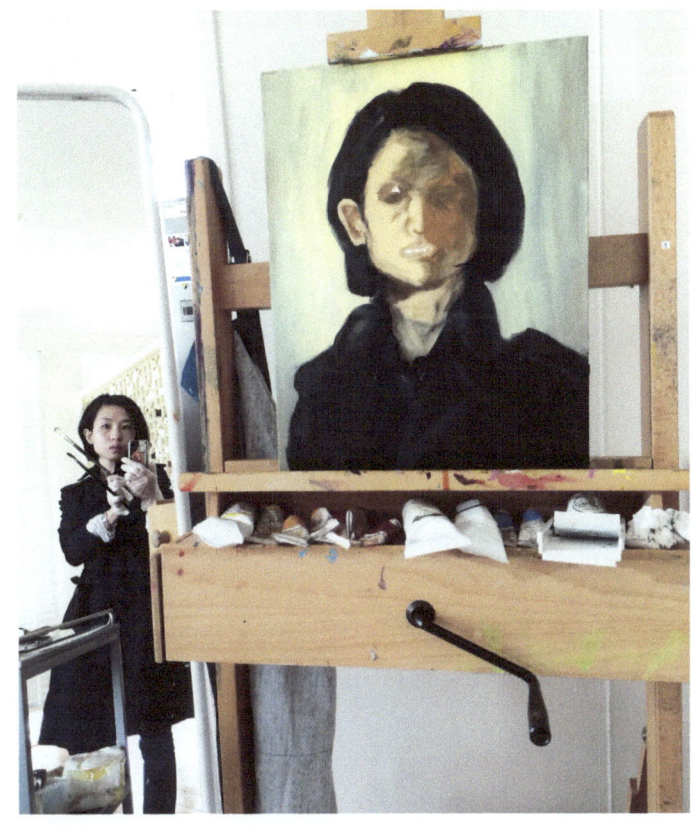

Now coming back to seeing yourself in the mirror, observe your own face, the bridge of your nose, the curve of your lips, the color of your cheeks etc., really see the details. While doing so, use that same kind of loving emotion to tell yourself "I love you", repeatedly.

Now try it. It only takes five minutes. I'll wait.

...

Have you done it? How do you feel?

Its effect on me was huge! It made me realised that I had completely forgotten what loving myself felt like, let alone how to love myself. It made me realised that I did not even see that myself was someone I needed to love, too.

The Bible says, "You shall love your neighbour as yourself." If we cannot extend love to ourselves, then how can we extend that love to our neighbours?

Now, we are going to take the mirror meditation to whole new levels. We are going to really see and know ourselves.

Wielding our paint tubes, brushes, canvases and a mirror, we have everything we need for the journey to self-discovery and self-compassion.

Shall we take off?

The Influence

In Chinese mythology, the mighty Pangu woke up from his 18,000 years of sleep, smashed the chaos with an axe, broke apart the formless world, and created the world of light and order as we know it.

I felt that Édouard Manet was the Pangu to art in the 19th century. He smashed the world not with an axe, but with his paint brush.

We may argue that he created chaos rather than order, that he destroyed "proper" form to create dashes of color. But we would agree that he had showed us a new world of freedom and light.

Matisse said of Manet, "He was the first to act on reflex and thus simplify the painter's business... expressing only what directly touched his senses."

For that, he was revolutionary. He marked a turning point in art history.

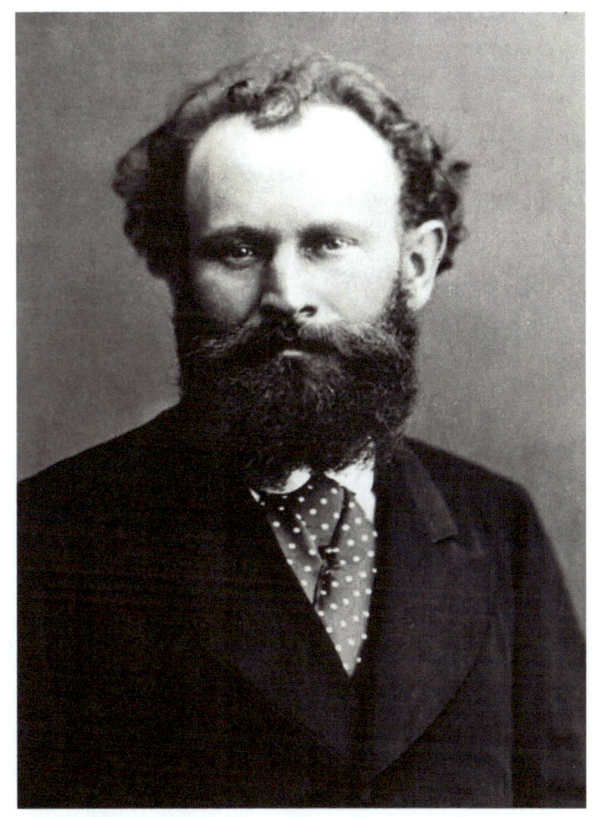

Édouard Manet, 1832–1883. Portrait by Nadar in 1874.

The Inspiration

As a woman, I am particularly interested in the women he painted.

Though Manet had quite a few women muses, two really stood out for me.

One was Victorine Meurent, a professional art model. The other was Berthe Morisot, a talented Impressionist artist herself.

Manet's portrait of "Berthe Morisot with a Bouquet of Violets" has been one of my favourite paintings of his. I like his use of black. I like that Berthe looks intelligent and classy.

That's exactly how I would like to see myself, an intelligent and classy artist, and an elite woman. Who's to argue with me?

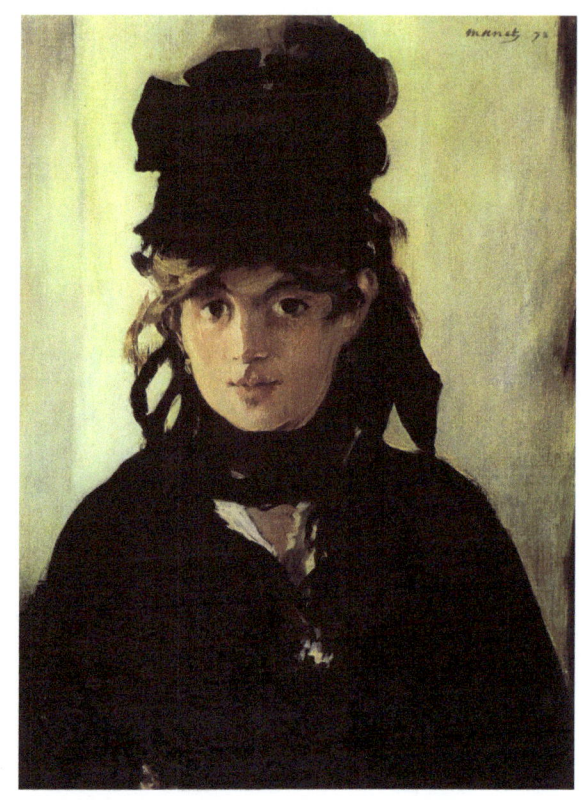

"Berthe Morisot with a Bouquet of Violets", oil, 15.9"x21.9", by Édouard Manet, 1872

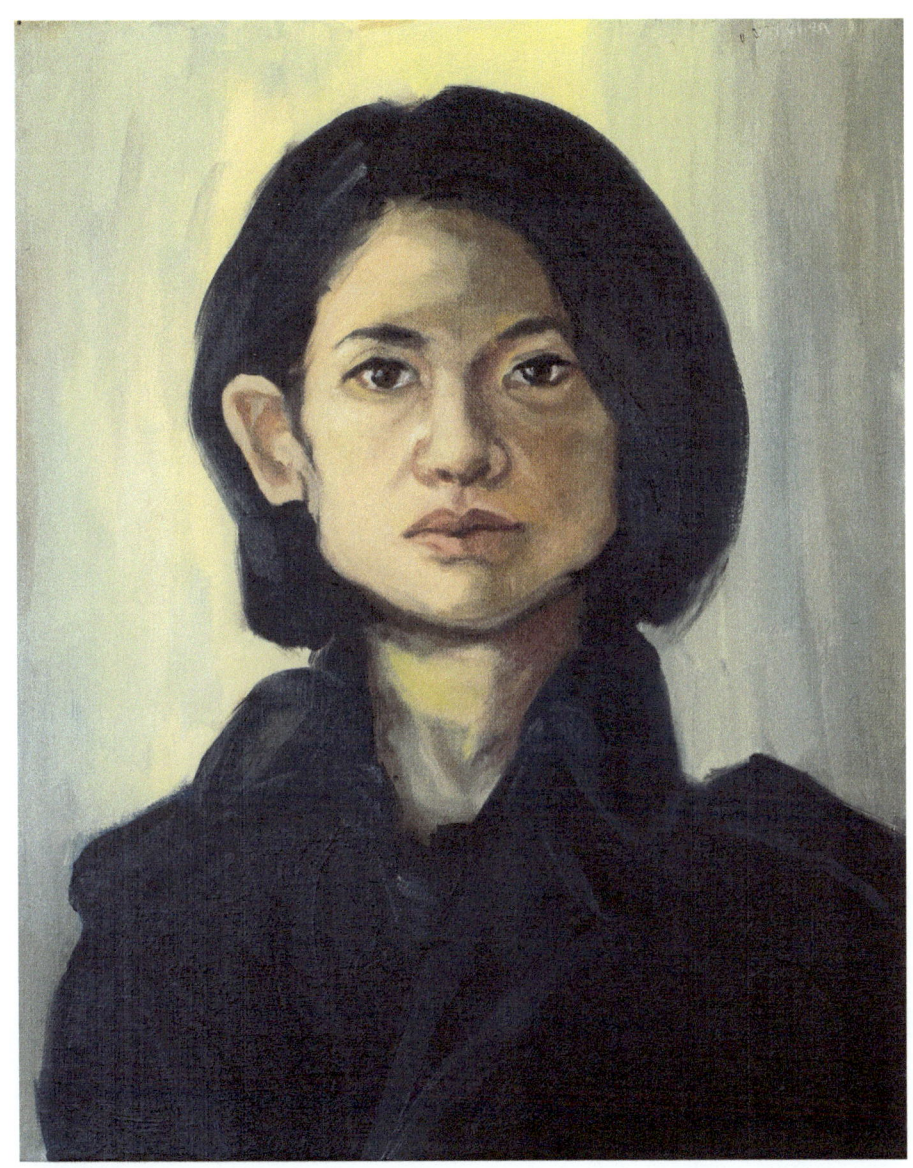

"If I Was His Muse", oil, 18"x14", by Lucy Chen, 2015

The Materials and The Palette

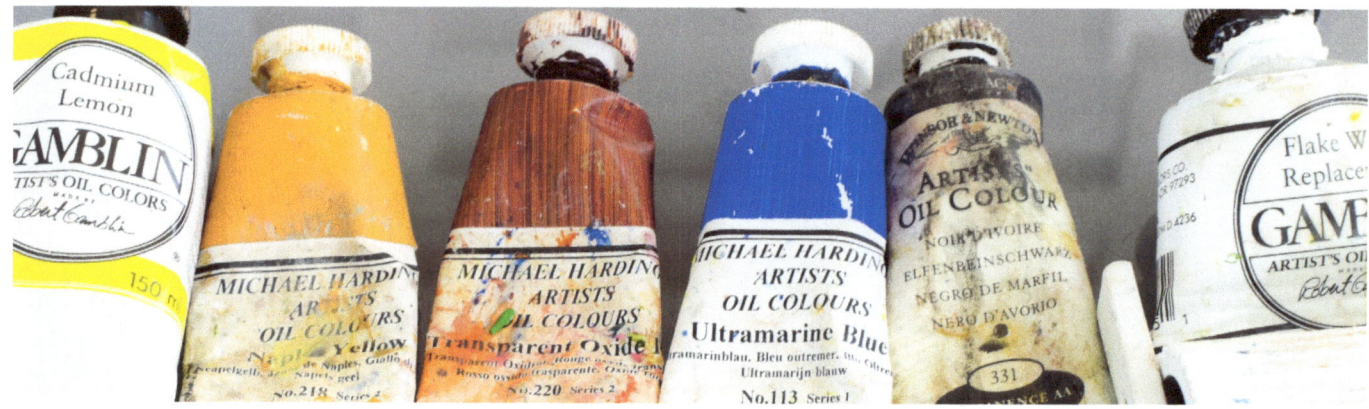

Édouard Manet is not your typical Impressionist. He was the artist who bridged Realism and Impressionism.

Manet abandoned the traditional way of building up layers and layers of paint with thin glazes, which took months if not years to create, and started painting alla prima.

His style has greatly influenced the Impressionists, and thus many see him as the father of Impressionism.

Unlike the other Impressionists who used vibrant colors in their works, Manet maintained the use of dark colors and strong contrasts.

When it comes to painting my Manet-inspired self portrait, here is a list of the materials I used:

Palette: Cadmium Lemon, Naples Yellow, Transparent Oxide Red, Ultramarine Blue, Ivory Black and Flake White Replacement

Brushes: Several bristle or synthetic flats and filberts, such as Rosemary & Co.'s Ivory range

Surface: Doubled primed stretched canvas

Others: Gamsol odourless mineral spirits, Neo Megilp, both by Gamblin, and paper towels

The Step-by-Step Process

1. SKETCH THE SHAPES

Use Ultramarine Blue with a touch of Transparent Oxide red thinned with Gamsol, sketch the outline of the portrait.

As both of these colors are transparent, they will not make your colors muddy as you start to layer other colors on top.

Make sure to keep your paint thin, sketch loosely, and wipe out unwanted marks with a paper towel.

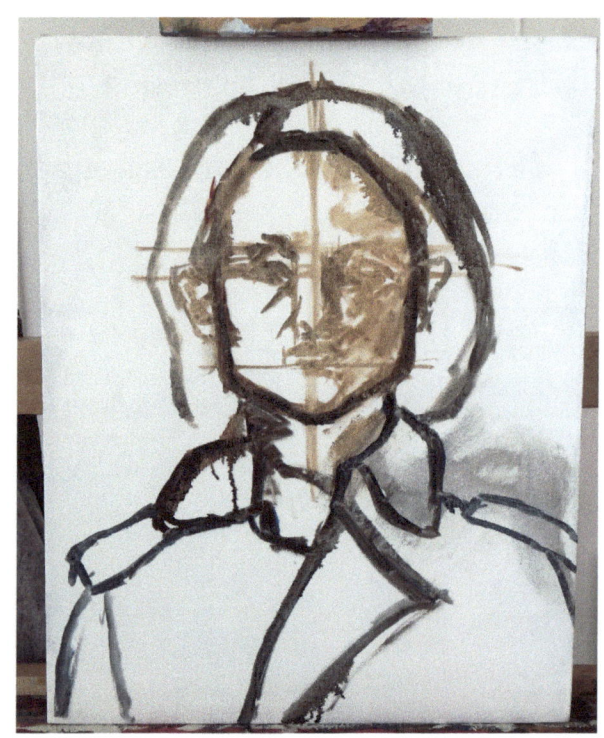

2. MASS IN THE FLESH TONES

Begin applying the flesh tones with a bristle or synthetic brush that can hold a good amount of paint and has good spring.

Use Naples Yellow and Flake White Replacement for the light side, and mass in Transparent Oxide Red for the dark side. Add touches of Ultramarine Blue.

Keep in mind that there are no exact fixed formula to mixing skin colors. Everyone has a different complexion, and it changes with the slightest alteration in the l hight and the surrounding environment. Your own feelings at the time of the painting can influence your color choices, too. It's only through trial and error will we arrive at the right mix for our painting.

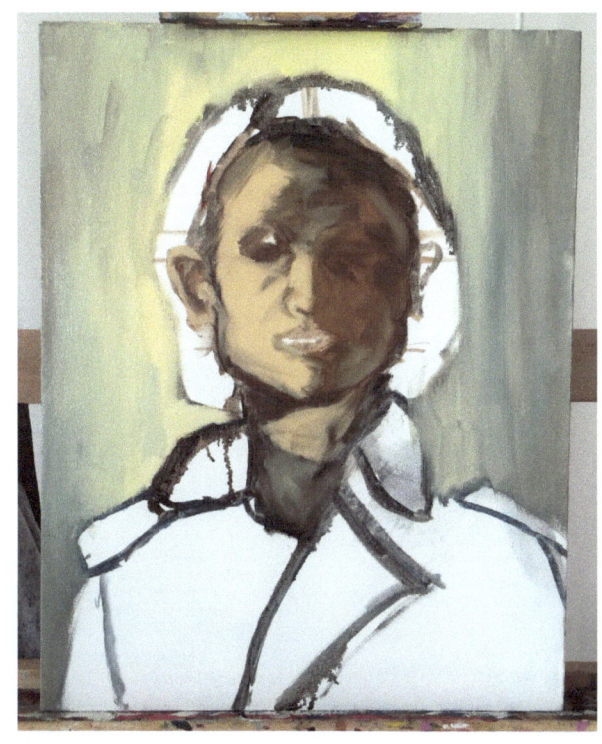

From this stage onwards, use paint straight from the tube, or bring in Neo Meglip to make the paint more spreadable while retaining the marks of the brushwork.

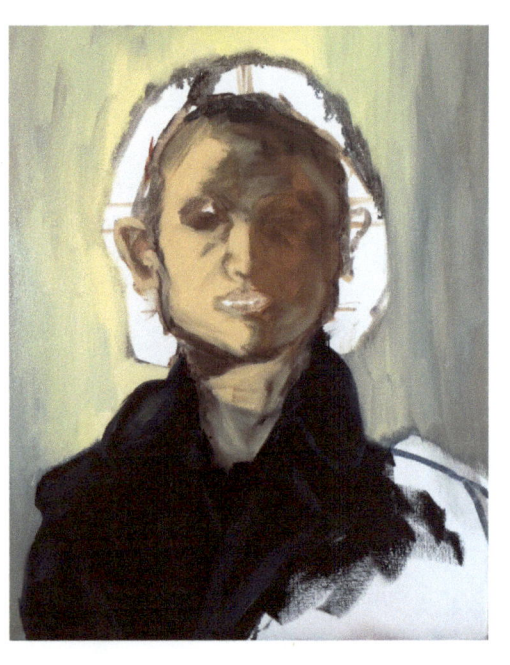

3. PAINT THE COAT AND THE BACKGROUND

Use a bigger brush to mass in the background with a mix of Cadmium Lemon and Flake White Replacement. Add touches of Ultramarine Blue or Naples Yellow to the mix to give variation.

Mass in the coat with Ivory Black, and simply bring in the light yellow color mix from the background to the highlights on the coat.

4. MASS IN THE HAIR

Use the same approach to paint the hair, keeping the brush strokes loose, and follow the flow of the hair. Keep the edges between the hair and forehead soft.

Unlike traditional painting where the darks are applied thinly, Manet used thick black paints. So feel free to push your black for what it's worth.

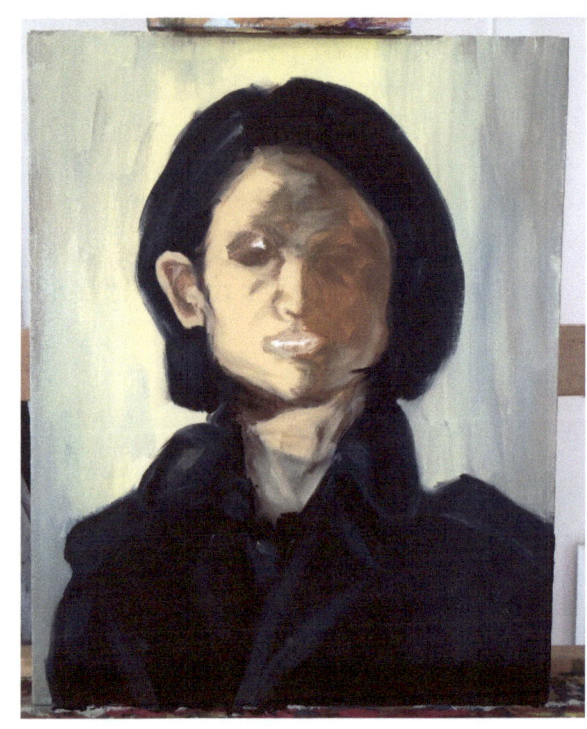

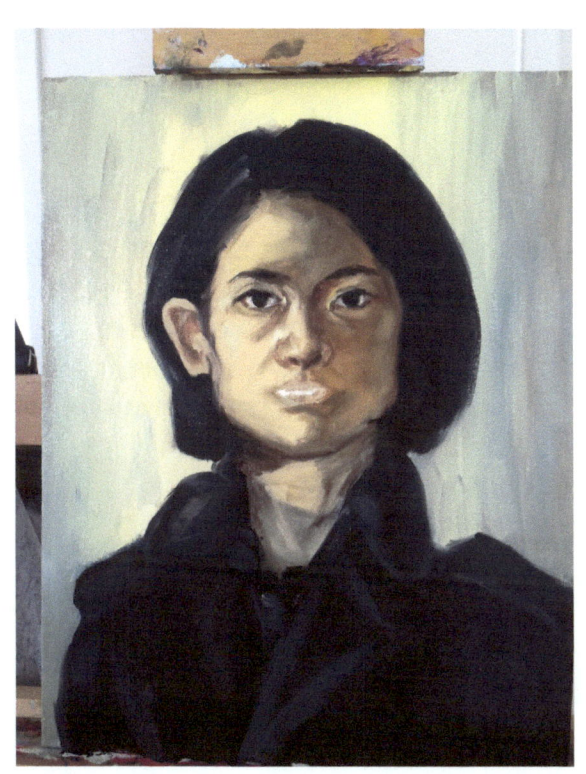

5. RENDER THE EYE

With a smaller synthetic brush, place the iris in the middle of the eye socket with Ivory Black. Mix a light grey color with Ultramarine Blue, Naples Yellow and Flake White Replacement for the white areas of the eye.

Don't cover the whole eye socket with the same shade of white. Make room for variations. Touch up with a Transparent Oxide Red mix to give definition.

6. REFINE TYE EYES

Apply a brown color mixed with Transparent Oxide Red and Naples Yellow to the iris, leaving the pupil in black. Add highlights with a cool off-white color.

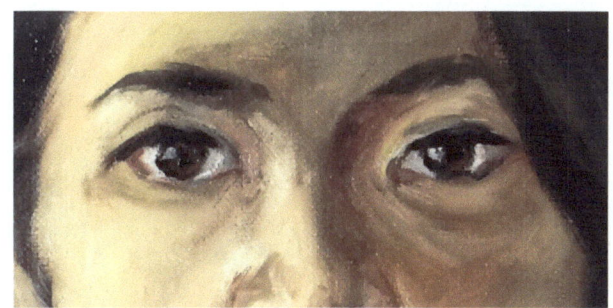

7. RENDER THE LIPS

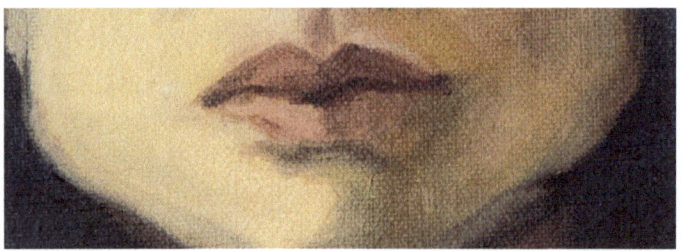

Add more Transparent Oxide Red to the flesh tone mix to make the color for the lips. It's important to decide on where to place the corners of the lips. Their placement plays an important role to the emotion a portrait conveys.

8. REFINE THE PORTRAIT AND ADD HIGHLIGHTS

Bring in some mid flesh tones to the dark side of the face in areas that are catching some light, and soften the edges in the process.

Add Cadmium Yellow with white to the highlights in the portrait.

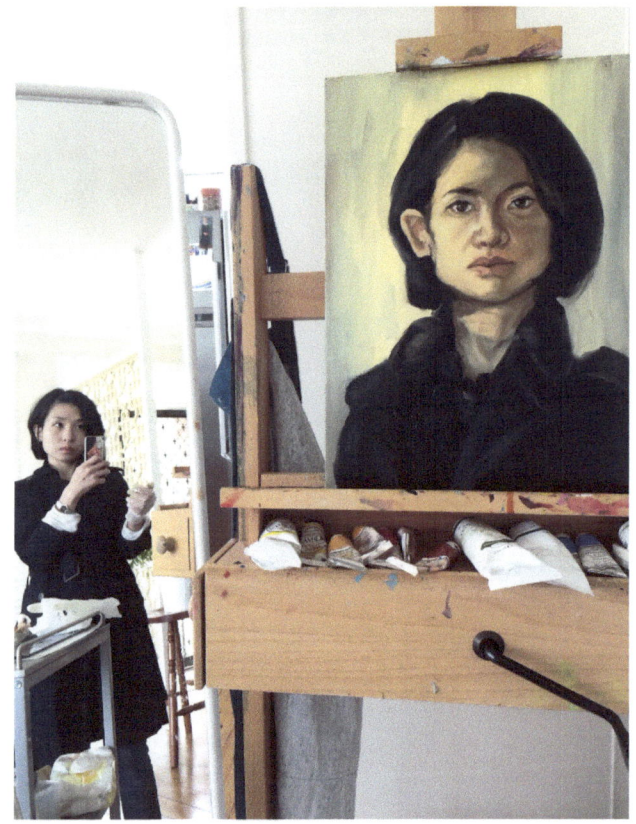

Afterword

Are you now ready to paint your own self portrait?

Don't worry about not getting it perfect.

Because whether we like it or not, our paintings will always come out imperfect.

But there is nothing to be ashamed of. We all struggle. Even the masters struggled.

Still, we are all worthy of love.

As Brené Brown says beautifully in her book The Gift of Imperfection,

"We cultivate love when we allow our most vulnerable and powerful selves to be deeply seen and known, and when we honour the spiritual connection that grows from that offering with trust, respect, kindness and affection."

So what are you waiting for? Get in front of a mirror, and start practicing seeing yourself deeply. Ready your brushes and paint, summon the power to create, and bring out that intelligent, classy and elite inner self in you!

Create and celebrate YOU!

Recommended Reading

Manet, Gilles Néret

The Judgement of Paris: The Revolutionary Decade That Gave the World Impressionism, Ross King

The Gifts of Imperfection, Brene Brown

Alla Prima II: Everything I Know about Painting and More, Richard Schmid

Art & Fear: Observations on the Perils and Rewards of Artmaking, David Bayles and Ted Orland

The Sacred Alone, Susannah Conway

About the Author

Lucy Chen is a China born, Australian grown, Sydney based artist. She discovered painting at the age of 29, three months before her second child's birth.

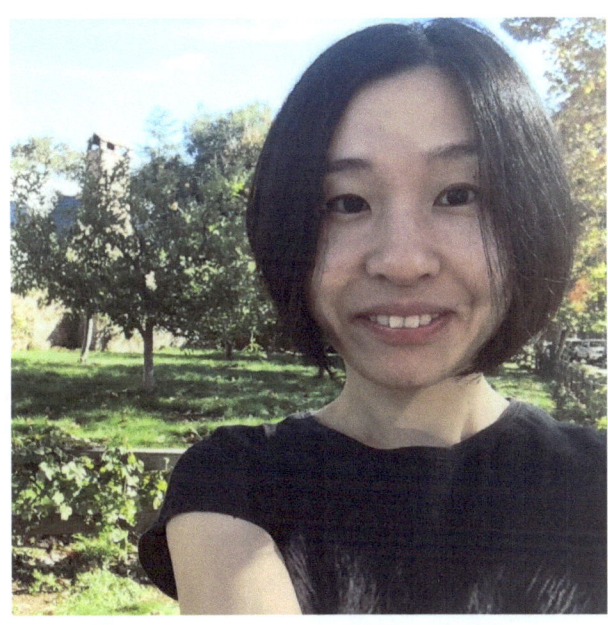

She lives in Sydney's north shore with her two little children, who share her studio as their play room.

She openly shares her creative process on her blog at http://lucychenfineart.com/blog.

And there are some bonus art videos for you, the reader of this book. Grab your FREE gift at: http://bit.ly/lcbook-bonus